21st Century Junior Library

Pliers

By Katie Marsico

CHERRY LAKE PUBLISHING * ANN ARBOR, MICHIGAN

CHERRY LAKE Publishing

Published in the United States of America by Cherry Lake Publishing
Ann Arbor, Michigan
www.cherrylakepublishing.com

Content Adviser: Roger McGregor, Director, Hannibal Career and Technical Center,
Hannibal, Missouri

Reading Adviser: Marla Conn, ReadAbility, Inc.

Photo Credits: Cover and page 20, ©Image Source Plus/Alamy; page 4, ©Winiki/Shutterstock,
Inc.; page 6, ©Planner/Shutterstock, Inc.; page 8, ©Odua Images/Shutterstock, Inc.; page 10,
©HakielBerry/Shutterstock, Inc.; page 12, ©Steve Heap/Shutterstock, Inc.; page 14, ©iStockphoto.
com/wakila; page 16, ©Auremar/Dreamstime.com; page 18, ©LUCARELLI TEMISTOCLE/
Shutterstock, Inc.; page 20, ©Image Source Plus/Alamy.

LIBRARY OF CONGRESS CATALOGING-IN-PUBLICATION DATA
Marsico, Katie, 1980–
 Pliers/by Katie Marsico.
    pages cm.—(Basic tools) (21st century junior library)
Audience: K to grade 3.
Includes bibliographical references and index.
 ISBN 978-1-62431-174-1 (lib. bdg.)—ISBN 978-1-62431-306-6 (pbk.)—
ISBN 978-1-62431-240-3 (e-book)
1. Pliers—Juvenile literature. I. Title.
TJ1201.T64M37 2014
621.9'92—dc23   2013007651

Cherry Lake Publishing would like to acknowledge the work of
The Partnership for 21st Century Skills.
Please visit www.p21.org *for more information.*

Printed in the United States of America
Corporate Graphics Inc.
July 2013
CLFA13

CONTENTS

Using pliers can make it easier to tighten or loosen a bolt.

What Are Pliers?

Have you seen someone loosen a bolt? A bolt is a metal pin or fastener. Did the person use only his or her fingers on the bolt? Or did he or she use pliers? Pliers are a hand tool. They **grip**, cut, bend, and **compress** objects.

Fulcrum

A pliers' two levers move on the fulcrum.

Pliers are made up of a pair of metal **levers**. These levers join at a fulcrum. The fulcrum is the main hinge, or pin. It supports the levers. The levers turn on the fulcrum.

Some people prefer to use pliers that have rubber on the handles.

The levers form long handles on one end. They meet as short jaws at the other. The fulcrum is between the handles and jaws. Some handles are covered in plastic or rubber. The jaws are usually flat and **serrated**.

Make a Guess!

Why are the handles on pliers coated with plastic or rubber? Think about gripping plastic or rubber. How is it different from gripping metal?

Squeezing the handles of pliers together makes the jaws close tightly on a nail or other object.

How Are Pliers Used?

A person first opens a pliers' handles. This opens the jaws. The person then closes the jaws around an object. Next, the person squeezes the handles together. The levers turn on the fulcrum. This squeezes the object between the pliers' jaws.

Jewelry makers use pliers to shape wires in their jewelry.

People use pliers to grip bolts, nails, and pins. Then they can loosen or tighten the objects. Pliers can also bend, twist, and straighten metal. **Electricians** use pliers a lot. Pliers can both cut and join electrical wires.

Ask Questions!

Talk to an electrician the next time you meet one. Ask how electricians use pliers on the job. Find out how electricians stay safe while fixing wiring with pliers.

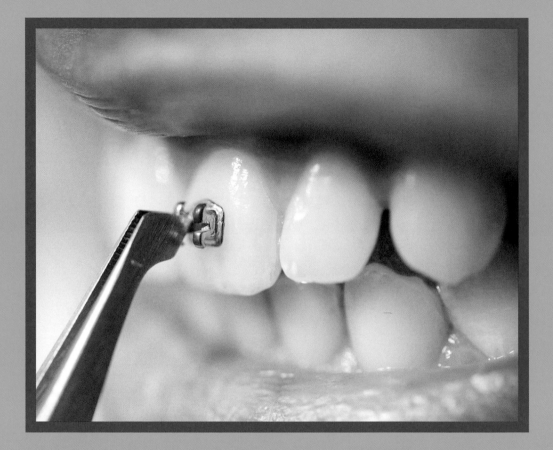

Dentists use special pliers to grip tiny parts in braces.

Doctors rely on special pliers. These tools grip items such as cotton balls. That way, doctors do not touch the items with their hands. Dentists use pliers, too. Pliers help tighten, loosen, and fix people's braces. Pliers can grip the tiny pieces of wire and metal in braces.

Slip-joint pliers can be adjusted to fit large or small bolts.

Different Kinds of Pliers

Not all pliers are the same. You have probably seen slip-joint pliers. Your parents might keep these pliers in a toolbox. Slip-joint pliers have a movable fulcrum. This allows the jaws to spread to different widths.

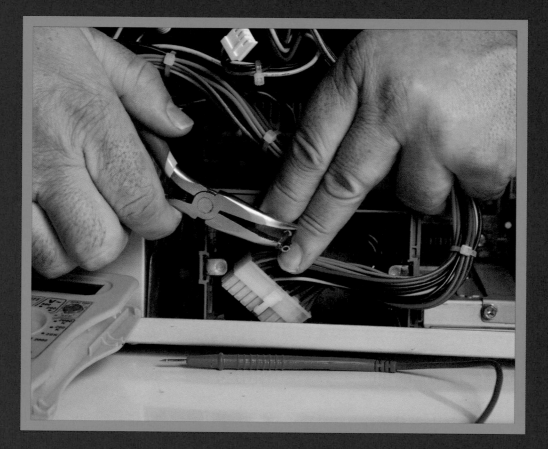

People often use needle-nose pliers when working with wires in computers.

The jaws of needle-nose pliers are long and thin. The jaws end in sharp points. Electricians use these pliers. They help bend and cut wires. They are great for working in tight spaces.

Bolt cutters can cut through thick chains and iron bars. Bolt cutters usually have long handles. Their jaws are short. But they are very strong.

You can use pliers in a lot of your own projects, such as fixing your bike.

Ask an adult to help you use pliers correctly. You may pinch yourself if you are not careful. Yet pliers are an important tool. You should learn to use them. They supply the extra squeeze to get the job done!

Think!

Think of some uses for pliers not mentioned in this book. Here is a hint: Everyone from plumbers to violin repairers work with this tool.

GLOSSARY

compress (kuhm-PRES) to press or flatten something in order to fit it into a smaller space

electricians (i-lek-TRISH-uhnz) people who install electrical systems and fix electrical equipment

grip (GRIP) to keep a tight hold on something

levers (LEV-urz) bars that turn on a fulcrum to move objects

serrated (SER-ay-tid) having a blade or edge like that of a saw

FIND OUT MORE

BOOKS

Hanson, Anders. *Pliers*. Edina, MN: ABDO, 2010.

Nelson, Robin. *What Do Pliers Do?* Minneapolis: Lerner, 2013.

WEB SITES

Canadian Centre for Occupational Health and Safety (CCOHS): Pliers and Wire Cutters
www.ccohs.ca/oshanswers/safety _haz/hand_tools/pliers.html
Find out about different kinds of pliers and see sketches of them.

How Stuff Works: Pliers
http://home.howstuffworks.com /pliers.htm
Learn more about how pliers work and how to use them safely.

INDEX

ABOUT THE AUTHOR

Katie Marsico is the author of more than 100 children's books. She lives in a suburb of Chicago, Illinois, with her husband and children.